No. 10. { Information for the]

THE SOUTHERN QUESTION.

THE BOURBON CONSPIRACY TO RULE OR DESTROY THE NATION.

CHAPTER I.

THE PRINCIPLES OF STATE SOVEREIGNTY ONLY SLUMBERING—CONTROL OF THE DEMOCRATIC PARTY NORTH ESSENTIAL TO ITS ASSERTION—AGENCIES EMPLOYED TO SECURE THIS END—THE REBELS WHO HAVE NOT YET SURRENDERED—DAVIS, BEN HILL AND OTHERS—THE SOUTHERN MAGAZINE—STATE OR NATIONAL SOVEREIGNTY—LIBERAL DEMOCRATS OF THE SOUTH.

SAVANNAH, GA., June 30, 1875.

It is believed that the leaders of the landed aristocracy, who assisted to inaugurate the rebellion, and did not surrender at Appomattox the cause for which they fought, have formed a conspiracy for the purpose of controlling the National Government, that they may "fix the status of the negro in our form of civilization" in the interest of the landed aristocracy. They will undoubtedly use fraud and force to accomplish their purposes. They are preparing for a desperate contest; it may be bloodless; it may be bloody. We watch the development of this conspiracy with the deepest interest. We fear that Northern Republicans do not know how formidable it is, and do not realize how great the danger is.

In 1861 the people of the North did not believe the nation was in danger until the war actually commenced. These conspirators are desperate political gamblers, and they play for a great stake. The cotton crop alone for the last eight years was about 25,045,771 bales, worth at least $2,296,377,585. Add to this the value of the rice, sugar and tobacco crops, and remember that most of this wealth was produced by negro labor, formerly owned by the landed aristocracy, of about 200,000 men, and the importance to them of controlling the labor of the negro may be realized.

THE MOVING PRINCIPLE OF JEFFERSON DAVIS' LIFE.

We are informed by Alfriend in his *Life of Jefferson Davis*, that after his defeat by Foote, the Union candidate for Governor of Mississippi, in 1851, "he was avowedly determined to devote his energies to the efficient organization of the States Rights party for future struggles. * * * His aim was to secure for the States Rights principle a moral and numerical support in the ranks of the Democracy, which should enable its friends to wield an appropriate influence upon the policy of that party." In ten years the "States Rights Party" controlled the Southern States, and its leaders, with Jefferson Davis at their head, attempted to destroy the nation and establish the Confederacy. In 1861 a majority of the Southern people were opposed to the policy of the slave aristocracy; but the latter were thoroughly organized, and, lead by able, wealthy, arrogant, desperate men, who would permit no opposition, they compelled the masses to obey their commands. Their power was displayed upon many hard-fought battle-fields.

THE SOUTH IN THE GREELEY CAMPAIGN.

When the war ended the landed aristocracy were poor, disheartened. and crushed. They had staked everything on the result of the war, and most of them had nothing left but their lands, which they expected would be taken from them. Toombs, and other leaders of influence, fled to Europe. Davis, Stephens, and others were imprisoned. The masses were willing to accept the terms which the victorious North might name, until Johnson betrayed the loyal cause. Then Toombs and his associates returned. Those who had been imprisoned were released. Ku-Klux Klans were organized, and the Congressional plan of reconstruction was opposed with great bitterness. Southern men of eminence who advised the people to accept the situation were denounced in the vilest manner. Republican leaders were murdered, and their families ostracized. Many of the Democratic leaders of the South were disheartened after the Presidential election in 1868. In 1872 a large majority were willing to accept any platform and any candidate for President that the leaders of their party at the North might present; but the ablest leaders of the State sovereignty party refused to support Greeley. For mere party success they cared nothing, save as it insured the triumph of the principles for which the South fought. As those principles were abandoned by the Democratic party, they were indifferent to the result, not caring whether Grant or Greeley was elected.

REORGANIZATION OF THE STATE SOVEREIGNTY PARTY.

It is believed that after Mr. Davis was released from confinement he "determined to devote his energies to the efficient" reorganization of the State Sovereignty Party "for future struggles," and that he has since been actively engaged in that work. He has visited different sections of the South, where he made speeches to arouse the masses, but secret organization has undoubtedly been his most important work. Alfriend says that in reply to the remark that the cause of the Confederacy was lost, Mr. Davis said: "It appears so. But the principle for which we contended is bound to reassert itself, though it may be at another time and in another form." Mr. Stephens, late Vice-President of the Confederacy, has rendered Mr. Davis valuable assistance. In 1867 he published a book entitled "*The War between the States*," which was written to prove that the South was right and the North was wrong in the late war. It has undoubtedly been the aim of the Bourbon leaders to secure for the State sovereignty principles a moral and numerical support in the ranks of the Democracy which will enable them to exercise a controlling influence upon the policy of that party. They undoubtedly have a comprehensive plan of secret organization. Since 1873 they have been preparing for the campaign of 1876. They have organized and marshaled their forces in a most skillful manner, and they have resorted to almost every means that human ingenuity could devise to accomplish their purposes. Social ostracism, villification, intimidation, force, fraud, murder—all have been used to control the governments of the Southern States, that the electoral vote of each may be cast for the Democratic candidate for President in 1876.

A POLITICAL, IF NOT REBELLIOUS, SOCIETY.

The Southern Historical Society is undoubtedly the organization that the leaders of the State Sovereignty Party are using "to secure for the States Rights principle a moral and numerical support in the ranks of the Democracy, which will enable its friends to wield an appropriate influence upon the policy of that party." That society was organized in 1869, in New Orleans, and Rev. Dr. Palmer, of the Presbyterian Church, made president. The public, however, knew but little of the society until it was reorganized by the Bourbon leaders in August, 1873, at the Montgomery Springs, Virginia. Then General Jubal Early was elected president. Since the re-organization of the society, its power has been felt, and now the Bourbons control the Democratic party in the Southern States, and will undoubtedly control the party in the nation.

General Wade Hampton, in an address delivered before the society in October, 1873, said:

"This society proposes to publish regularly and systematically all contribudions which elucidate the truth, reflect the glory, and maintain the principles involved in the late war, and it calls upon all who are not lost to honor to aid in this laudable undertaking. It wishes to enroll, not only every true man, but every true woman in its ranks."

Henry Ewbank, the general agent of the society, in an address to the people of Georgia, in January, 1874, said:

"Having enrolled among its members the true exponents of Southern honor and intelligence, it will necessarily possess a vitality and exert a moral influence through the whole South, which will steadily and irresistibly expand into an antagonism powerful to repel the insidious advance of those vicious principles which are now so fearfully undermining the civilization of the North. * * * In view of the vital issues involved, and of the noble results attainable through the effective operation of this society, I dare not doubt the success of my efforts in Georgia in its behalf."

The *Southern Magazine*, the official organ of the society, in a leading editorial, published in December, 1874, said:

"We have, as our readers know, abstained almost entirely from discussing parties or politics in these pages. They have these abundantly treated in the daily and weekly press, and we have deemed it better that this magazine, which is meant for the hours of leisure, should lead them into other fields of thought. But the great political revolution which is now in progress, is of such momentous importance, and is so far from being a mere party triumph, that it should not pass without some notice from us. It is not, we say, the mere victory of one party over another. * * * * It is the opening of the people's eyes, North and South, East and West, to the tendency and result of those doctrines which have for fourteen years predominated in this country, and against which the Southern States protested by pen, and tongue, and ballot, so long as these availed, and when these availed not, by the sword. * * * It cannot be long, we think, before thinking-men at the North perceive what has been our thesis all along, that in the late war of the States the South was defending their cause as well as her own. * * * The true policy of Conservatives is not (if that be possible) to blot out the past, but to lead the country, which has gone widely astray, back to the true paths, and to go forward in them. Let us find the road from which we have wandered—the road which led to such prosperity. * * * Let us find it once more and follow it into the future."

The *Southern Magazine* truly represents the views and policy of the Bourbons who control the Southern Historical Society.

STATE SOVEREIGNTY VS. NATIONAL SUPREMACY.

All Democratic leaders of influence in this section assume that the "coming great struggle" is to be between State sovereignty and national supremacy. Mr. Stephens, says: "The coming great struggle is to be between Constitutionalism and Centralism in the United States." In other words, between State sovereignty and national supremacy, Senator Gordon, says: "We should insist upon the right of the States to manage for themselves their own internal affairs. Without this right were fully protected, and its maintenance guaranteed, I would not give a cent for any victory." In other words, he would not give a cent for any victory that does not secure State sovereignty. Mr. Benjamin H. Hill, says: "The great final struggle to settle the question whether constitutional liberty on this continent shall be continued or not, is to be fought in 1876. Can it be successfully fought with the ballot? * * * If we fail at the ballot-box in 1876, by reason of force, a startling question will present itself to the American people. * * * I tell you, my friends, there is no peace for this country until Radicalism is crushed; not only crushed, but despised; not only despised, but made infamous forever throughout America. If we must have war—if we cannot preserve this Constitution and constitutional government by the ballot; * * * if folly and wickedness—if inordinate love of power shall decree that America must save her Constitution by blood, let it come. I am ready.

But let one thing be distinctly understood, that if another war should come, we of the South will rally under the old flag of our fathers. It always was our flag. We were never faithless to it, and our enemies were never faithful to it." Stephens, Hill and Gordon truly represent the Bourbon Democracy of Georgia, who now control the State.

BEN. HILL AND HIS CONGRESSIONAL DISTRICT.

The election of Mr. Hill to Congress from the Ninth District of Georgia, to fill a vacancy caused by the death of Hon. Garnet McMillan, was a significant event. He is one of the most extreme Bourbon leaders in the State, and undoubtedly the ablest orator from the South in public life. He was a Senator in the Confederate Congress, and Chairman of the Judiciary Committee. It is said that his services were so valuable to Mr. Davis, that he called him "My right arm." Since the close of the war, he has been the most prominent Democrat in Georgia. His "war speech" from which I have quoted, made on the 20th of January last, before a convention of ex-Confederate soldiers, resident in Georgia, was received with "wild applause," and greatly increased his popularity with the Bourbon Democracy. They manifested a deep interest in the contest in the Ninth District, and even Toombs, who had been his bitter enemy for many years, offered to canvas the district in his behalf. One part of the district is composed of the mountainous counties of Northeastern Georgia, where the inhabitants are white farmers, who formerly owned but few slaves, and now cultivate their own lands. In the rest of the district there was a large slave population. There, the landed aristocracy now control the Democratic party. The Democratic convention to nominate a candidate for Congress met on the 14th of April, and adjourned on the 21st, without making a nomination. The two-third rule was adopted, and under it the delegates balloted 414 times. Hill was supported by 28 delegates, the representatives of the landed aristocracy. Mr. Bell, his opponent, the candidate of the white farmers of Northeastern Georgia, received thirty-three votes. Hill's friends were determined that no one should be nominated, if they could not nominate him, as they believed they could elect him if no nomination was made. During the canvas Hill took "high Democratic ground." He charged his principal opponent, a Democrat, with being a "Radical" because he did not oppose the thirteenth, fourteenth, and fifteenth amendments to the Constitution of the United States. Two candidates, both Democrats, opposed him, but his majority over both was 2,180.

STATE SOVEREIGNTY.

The doctrine of State sovereignty was formerly used to protect slavery and all the evils incident to that institution. Democratic statesmen held that the States were sovereign; Republican statesmen believed that the nation—the United States—was sovereign. The immediate cause of the late war was the attempt of the Southern States to secede from the nation; but the attempt to secede was made that a government might be established to protect slavery. Slavery was the cause that produced the different and opposite modes of construing the Constitution of the United States, the different and opposite modes of considering our form of general government. The soldiers of the Confederacy fought for the independence of their States. The Union soldiers fought for the nation. The stars and bars—the flag of the Confederacy—was the symbol of State sovereignty; the stars and stripes—the flag of the nation—was the symbol of national supremacy; but behind one stood slavery; behind the other freedom. The contest was between slavery and freedom. It is evident that many Southern leaders have not surrendered the political dogmas that brought on the war, and were settled by it, as the North supposed. The doctrine of State sovereignty is now advocated because the Bourbons wish to control labor.

THE LIBERAL ELEMENT IN THE DEMOCRATIC PARTY.

It is true that many men at the South who are nominally Democrats are not Bourbons, and it is believed that a large majority of the voters are opposed to the Bourbon policy, but as the questions that have divided the people of the South since the war, have related to "the status of the negro in our form of civilization," parties have divided on the "color line:" one party being practically a white man's party, and the other a negro party. The Bourbons seek to keep that the dividing line between parties, that they may control the Southern States by uniting the whites in opposition to the Republican party. The educated class of the South was formerly interested in slavery, therefore most of the professional men and the ablest public speakers are Bourbons. The Bourbons control the Democratic press, and they control "society." By social ostracism, denunciation, and vilification, they have prevented the liberal element from joining the Republican party. But that element is increasing in numbers, and it is believed that the Liberals will not continue much longer to support the Democratic party. They may, and most of them probably will do so, until after the next Presidential election, when, if the Republican candidate for President is elected, they will undoubtedly publicly oppose the Bourbons. Then a powerful Republican party may be organized in every Southern State, led by able, honest, skillful men.

The South is now comparatively quiet; but it is the quiet that precedes a storm. The bad element is more easily controlled than formerly, and the organization of the Bourbons is so perfect that it is not necessary for them now to "fire the Southern heart." That, however will be done at the proper time.

A GEORGIA REPUBLICAN.

CHAPTER II.

THE COMING GREAT STRUGGLE BETWEEN STATE SOVEREIGNTY AND NATIONAL SUPREMACY—HON. A. H. STEPHENS THE LEADER IN THE NEW MOVEMENT.

SAVANNAH, GA., August 23, 1875.

Although slavery was the cause of the late war, the conflict arose from different and opposing ideas as to the nature of the general government. The slave lords who ruled the South held to the heresy of State sovereignty; the people of the North believed that the nation was supreme. But State sovereignty and Constitutional liberty were used as synonymous terms by the crafty leaders of the slave power, who pretended that the South was fighting for liberty, and they have taught the people that liberty was overthrown when Lee surrendered. For thirty years the people of the South were carefully educated in the doctrine of State sovereignty, and for four years they fought to maintain that doctrine. Some have supposed that when the South laid down its arms, it acknowledged the defeat of the opinions for which it was contending. Many of the people undoubtedly did, but the Bourbon leaders did not, and they are preparing to make another great struggle for the same opinions.

JEFFERSON DAVIS.

As before stated, Jefferson Davis, late President of the Confederacy, has affirmed, since the close of the war, that the principle for which the South contended was bound to reassert itself.

SPEECH OF ALEXANDER H. STEPHENS BEFORE THE GEORGIA LEGISLATURE, ON THE 22D OF FEBRUARY, 1866.

Alexander H. Stephens, late Vice-President of the Confederacy, said in a speech, delivered before the Georgia Legislature, on the 22d of February, 1866:

"Whatever may be said of the loyalty or disloyalty of any in the late most lamentable conflict of arms, I think I may venture safely to say that there was on the part of the great mass of the people of Georgia and of the entire South, *no disloyalty* to the principles of the Constitution of the United States. * * * With us, it was simply a question as to where our allegiance was due in the maintenance of these principles—which authority was paramount in the last resort—State or Federal. As for myself I can affirm that no sentiment of disloyalty to these great principles of self-government, recognized and embodied in the Constitution of the United States, ever beat or throbbed in breast or heart of mine. To their maintenance my whole soul was ever enlisted; and to this end my whole life has heretofore been devoted, and will continue to be the rest of my days—God willing. * * * Whatever differences existed amongst us, arose from differences as to the best and surest means of securing these great ends, which was the object of all. It was with this view and for this purpose, secession was tried. That has failed. * * * Our only alternative now is either to give up all hope of Constitutional liberty, or retrace our steps, and to look for its vindication and maintainance in the forums of reason and justice, instead of on the arena of arms. In the court and halls of legislation, instead of on the field of battle. * * *

"We are not without an encouraging example on this line in the history of the mother country. * * * The truest friends of liberty in England once, in 1642, abandoned the forums of reason, and appealed as we did, to the sword, as the surest means, in their judgment, of advancing their cause. * * * But the end was the reduction of the people of England to a worse state of oppression than they had been in for centuries. They retraced their steps. * * * The House of Commons and the House of Lords were henceforth the theatres of their operations. * * * The result was, that in less than thirty years, all their ancient rights and privileges which had been lost in the civil wars, with new securities, were re-established. * * * "May we not indulge hope, even in the alternative before us now, from this great example of restoration, if we but do as the friends of liberty there did? This is my hope, my only hope."

STEPHENS' PLAN TO REGAIN THE "LOST CAUSE."

"According to Stephens' reasoning, the people of the South in their attempt to destroy the nation were not disloyal, but they were fighting for liberty; indeed, they were "the truest friends of liberty." As they failed to establish liberty by secession, they must "look for its vindication and maintainance in the forums of reason and justice." Thus they may regain all their ancient rights and privileges which were lost in the civil war, with new securities. To that end the people of the South should be educated to cherish the "lost cause," that the South may regain its "liberties" as the mother country did. To that work he promised to dedicate the remainder of his days. Thus far he has kept his promise.

STEPHENS' LIFE DEVOTED TO THE ADVOCACY OF SLAVERY AND STATE SOVEREIGNTY.

Mr. Stephens' life has been devoted to the advocacy of slavery and State sovereignty. He entered public life in 1836 as a representative in the Georgia legislature, elected on the "States Rights Ticket." He entered Congress in 1843, a "State Rights Whig," and returned in 1859, a "States Rights Democrat." In 1850, he assisted to draw up, and earnestly advocated the famous "Georgia platform, which declared that the State of Georgia "will, and ought to, resist, even (as a last resort,) to a disruption of every tie which binds her to the Union, any future act of Congress abolishing slavery in the District of Columbia without the consent and petition of the slaveholders thereof; or, any act abolishing slavery in places within the slave-holding States purchased by the United States for the erection of forts, magazines, dock-yards, navy-yards, and other like places; or, in any act suppressing the slave trade between slave holding States; or, in any refusal to admit as a State any territory applying, because of the existence of slavery therein; or in any act prohibiting the introduction of slaves into the territories of Utah and New Mexico; or in any act repealing or materially modifying the laws now in force for the recovery of fugitive slaves."

In 1840, 1844, and 1848 he supported the candidates of the Whig party for the Presidency. But, in 1852, he refused to support General Scott because he was not sufficiently sound on the slavery question. In 1856 he advocated the election of Buchanan, and in 1860 the election of Douglas.

STEPHENS' GREAT UNION (?) SPEECH OF 1860.

He delivered his celebrated Union (?) speech before the Legislature of Georgia in November 1860. He said that he stood on the "Georgia platform," as he had always done since its adoption, and, if the Republicans attempted by an act of Congress to exclude the slaveholders from the territories with their slave property, no man would be more willing or ready than he to disrupt every tie which bound the States together. But he advised the people to wait until the Republican policy was adopted, before they tried secession. The "secessionists" favored immediate secession. In a letter to a strong secessionist in New York, he gave the following reason for advocating the policy of delay:

"The great and leading object aimed at by me at Milledgeville, was to produce harmony on a right line of policy. If worst comes to worst, as it may, and our State has to quit the Union, it is of the utmost importance that all our people should be united cordially in this cause. This, I feel confident, can only be effected on the line of policy I indicated."

TOOMBS AND STEPHENS.

Toombs and Stephens have been bosom friends from boyhood. They were born in adjoining counties; they entered public life about the same time, and were in accord politically until 1860. Then Toombs was a violent secessionist.

Stephens was a "Union man," *so-called*. A large number of Georgians were opposed to secession from principle. Toombs was the leader of the secessionists. Stevens of the Union men. Toombs fought for secession. Stephens for the Union *on the "Georgia platform," "to produce harmony on a right line of policy."* The secessionists triumphed, and Stephens led the Union men into the movement, and was rewarded with the Vice-Presidency of the Confederacy. Again, he and Toombs were bosom friends, as they now are.

STEPHENS' LIFE WORK.

The statement that his whole soul was ever enlisted in the maintainance of the principle of State sovereignty, and, to that end, his whole life had been devoted, *and would continue to be the rest of his days*, was more significant than was generally supposed. The mantle of Calhoun has fallen upon his shoulders. He is now the foremost Southern politician; the most adroit man in public life from the South, and he undoubtedly possesses more influence than any other Southern man. He utters no harsh words, and he is the more dangerous on that account. There is an appearance of candor in what he says, that pleases even an opponent.

STEPHENS' ADROITNESS.

Cleveland in his life of Stephens, says:

"He has been often heard to say, that his views in consenting to take part in the Hampton Roads Conference can never be fully understood without a knowledge of the true objects contemplated by the authors of that mission. These he has never disclosed."

It is believed that his views upon public measures of importance can never be fully understood by those who listen to his talk and to his speeches without a knowledge of the real objects contemplated by him. In 1860 many persons believed him to be a Union man. But, in his letter to the New York secessionists he disclosed the true object contemplated by him:—"To produce harmony on a right line of policy," before secession was attempted. He undoubtedly disclosed, in his speech of December, 1866, the true object now contemplated by him—to regain the "lost cause." In a recent conversation with a correspondent of the Savannah *News*, he said:

"A wise general reserves the full strength of his army for the actual conflict, and seldom wastes it in efforts of a doubtful character for the mere purpose of frightening the enemy. I have long held to this opinion, and, as a journalist of twenty years' experience, I am fully convinced that much of the disaster which has overtaken the Democratic and Conservative party has been owing to a too early and general discussion of public measures and public men. When the real issue is made, in most cases, the enemy is fully prepared to meet it, as all the weakness of our cause has been laid open for months or years, and the plan of operation fully understood. In politics, as in war, the less the opposing forces know of our plans and puposes, except at the last moment, the better for our cause, and the greater the chances of sucess on our part."

HIS "DEEP GAME."

Some have supposed that because he has frequently spoken of the President in complimentary terms, and has not, as a rule, abused Republicans; that because he has voted for and defended some measures supported by Republicans, he is not in sympathy with the Bourbon Democracy. A writer in the Augusta *Chronicle and Sentinel*, the principal Democratic paper in his district, thus defends him from the assaults of those Democrats who do not fully understand his policy:

"Why is it that the thoughtless and the malicious are so anxious to impair the influence, and thwart the labors of the Great Commoner? Why are we not willing to trust him? Has he ever deceived us? Is he not playing a deep game for the salvation of the South? If he can control Grant, and induce him to accept a platform for his candidacy next year, why should we let our personal prejudices outweigh what should be our desire for the general welfare?"

The "deep game" which Mr. Stephens is playing is, undoubtedly, the concealing from the people of the North the true objects contemplated by him, while he prepares for the "coming great struggle between the Constitution and centralism in the United States." He thus defends himself from the charge of infidelity to "true Democratic principles," made by the Savannah *News*, in a letter which he recently wrote to that paper:

"If the real object and purpose of these imputations against my fidelity to true Democratic principles, be not barely a prelude to a contemplated open war upon me and my known position in the coming great struggle between constitutionalism and centralism in the United States, why, let me ask you, am I not only thus assailed in your paper upon charges so groundless, but made the special object of assault for my course upon the repeal of the act of March, 1873, increasing the pay of members of Congress?"

STEPHENS' PATIENCE, PERSEVERANCE, AND SAGACITY.

We can but admire the patience, perseverance, and sagacity with which, since 1866, he has pushed his life work. When others were willing to "accept the situation," he was preparing for the "coming great struggle." "We tried secession and failed," he said: "Now we will look for the vindication of our cause in the forums of reason and justice." His speech before the Georgia Legislature, in 1866, was soon followed by the publication of his life, the principal object in the publication of which appeared to be to lay before the people his ablest speeches and letters in favor of slavery and State sovereignty, and to make known his plan for regaining the "lost cause." In 1868 the first volume of *The War between the States* was issued, and, in 1870, the second volume was published for the purpose of proving the North was wrong and the South right in the late war. In 1871 he assumed control of the Atlanta *Sun*, which he edited and published until July, 1873, for the purpose of advocating the cause of State sovereignty, and preparing the people to again fight for that cause.

In August, 1873, the Southern Historical Society was organized "to publish regularly and systematically all contributions which elucidate the truth, reflect the glory, and maintain the principles involved in the late war." Since the organization of that society, Mr. Stephens' *public* labors in favor of the Confederacy have been slight, in comparison to what they were before that time. In 1872 he published a school history of the United States, to educate the children of the South in the heresy of State sovereignty.

He refused to support Greeley in 1872, because he was opposed to the doctrine of State sovereignty. Now the Southern Democracy controlled by the Bourbon leaders, stand on the platform of Davis, Stephens, and Toombs, and they are preparing for the coming great struggle between State sovereignty and National supremacy.

A GEORGIA REPUBLICAN.

CHAPTER III.

DAVIS, STEPHENS, AND TOOMBS, THE MOST INFLUENTIAL LEADERS OF THE SOUTHERN DEMOCRACY—THE SOUTHERN HISTORICAL SOCIETY—ITS PURPOSES, AS EXPLAINED BY GENERAL WADE HAMPTON.

SAVANNAH, GA., August 25, 1875.

Those who have not recently studied Southern politics with care will perhaps be surprised at the assertion that Davis, Stephens, and Toombs are now the most influential leaders of the Southern Democracy. There was a time since the close of the war, when their influence with the masses, as well as with the leaders, was slight; but the Southern Democracy is now controlled by those who advocate their policy.

BEN HILL ON DAVIS, STEPHENS, AND TOOMBS.

In 1871, Ben Hill said to a correspondent of the New York *Herald:*

"There will be an attempt very likely by Bob Toombs and Stephens to drive men of my stripe out of the Democracy. * * * I am confident that Toombs and the rest of the fire-eaters have no very great strength among the people."

In August, 1871, he said to a correspondent of the Knoxville (Tennessee) *Chronicle:*

"I have hopes that the Democracy will triumph this fall in Maine, Pennsylvania, Ohio, and California. If they do, the New Departure will be the main plank in the platform of 1872, and our success assured. In this event Toombs, Stephens, and Davis will be obliged either to formally leave the party or to acquiesce in the New Departure. * * * If we are defeated this year Toombs, Stephens, and Davis will be elated and strengthened. They will be defeated, however, as the South cannot and will not be lead by them." Now Hill himself, is lead by them: indeed he is one of the ablest advocates of their Bourbon policy, as much of a fire-eater as Toombs.

HILL AND STEPHENS.

Hill is a demagogue who panders to the people for votes. Stephens is the greatest thinker in the South, a leader and a teacher of the people. His contempt for the Democratic leaders of the North was recently manifested by him in a letter to the Savannah *News.* A writer in that paper censured him for his vote in the last Congress to take up the report of the committee on Louisiana affairs, because he was found voting "against the parliamentary tactics of the Democrats," and he replied:

"Wise and sagacious leaders of the Democracy of the Union think you were with those who planned such 'parliamentary tactics?' Heaven forbid that I should ever be found following such leaders when public liberty is at stake, and Heaven forbid that the cause of the true Democracy of the United States should ever be committed for guidance and control to the hands of the authors of such tactics."

Although Mr. Stevens has not publicly advocated the Confederate cause as zealously since July, 1873, as before that time, yet in his speech in Congress in opposition to the Civil Rights bill, January 5, 1874, and in his recent Fourth of July oration at Atlanta, he presented with his accustomed adroitness the arguments in favor of State sovereignty. It has not been necessary for him to devote as much time to the advocacy of that cause as he did formerly, for, in August, 1873, the Southern Historical Society entered upon that work.

THE SOUTHERN HISTORICAL SOCIETY.

The organization of the Southern Historical Society was an important step in the struggle between State sovereignty and national supremacy. Delegates representing twelve Southern States participated in the organization. Generals Beauregard, Early, and Fitzhugh Lee, Admiral Semmes and Governor Letcher were leading spirits. "President" Davis was also present. The minutes of the convention, published in the *Southern Magazine*, the official organ of the society, January, 1874, give the following account of his reception:

THE RECEPTION OF "PRESIDENT DAVIS."

AUGUST 16, 1873.

* * * "Governor Letcher," the president of the convention, "gave notice of the expected arrival of President Davis, and suggested the propriety of an adjournment of the convention till Monday, and the appointment of a committee to receive the President.

"On motion of General Beauregard, the chair appointed a committee composed of the following gentlemen: General Beauregard, Admiral Semmes, General Early, General Lilly, and General T. T. Mumford. * * *

"MONDAY, August 18, 1873.

* * * "Admiral Semmes then presented to the convention President Davis. The convention received him standing."

"Governor Letcher in a short address cordially welcomed President Davis, who made an appropriate acknowledgment in an address of a few moments to the convention."

THE OFFICERS OF THE SOUTHERN HISTORICAL SOCIETY.

The following gentlemen were elected the officers of the Southern Historical Society:

President—General Jubal Early, of Virginia.

Vice-President—Hon. R. M. T. Hunter, of Virginia.

Secretary and ex-officio Treasurer—Colonel G. W. Mumford, of Virginia.

Vice-Presidents of States—General Isaac R. Trumble, Md.; Governor Zebulon B. Vance, N. C.; General M. C. Butler, S. C.; General A. H. Colquitt, Ga.; Admiral R. Semmes, Ala.; Colonel W. Call, Fla.; General Wm. T. Martin, Miss.; General J. B. Hood, La.; Colonel T. M. Jack, Texas; Hon. A. H. Garland, Ark.; Governor Isham G. Harris, Tenn.; General J. S. Marmaduke, Mo.; General S. B. Buckner, Ky.; W. W. Corcoran, D. C.

The head-quarters of the society was established at the State House, Richmond, Virginia, late the capitol of the Confederacy.

THE PURPOSES OF THE SOCIETY—SPEECH OF GENERAL HAMPTON.

The purposes of the society were explained at length by General Wade Hampton in a speech, made before the society, October 29, 1873, from which I make the following extract:

"As it was the duty of every man to devote himself to the service of his country in the great struggle which has just ended so disastrously, not only to the South, but to the cause of Constitutional government under Republican institutions in the new world; so now, when that country is prostrate in the dust, weeping for her dead who died in vain to save her liberties, every patriotic impulse should urge her surviving children to vindicate the great principles for which she fought. * * * These are the imperative duties imposed upon us of the South; and the chief peril of the times is, that, in our despair at the evil that has fallen on us, we forget those obligations to the eternal principles for which we fought; to the martyred dead who gave up their lives for their principles; * * * and to our children who should be taught to cling to them with unswerving fidelity. If those who are to come after us, and to whose hands the destinies of our country are soon to be committed, are properly instructed in the theory and practice of Republican institutions; if they are *made* to comprehend the origin, progress, and culmination of that great controversy between the antagonistic sections of this continent, which began in the convention of 1787, and ended, for the time being, at Appomattox in 1865, they cannot fail to see that truth, right, justice were on the side of their fathers, and they will surely strive to bring back to the Republic those cardinal principles on which it was founded, and on which alone it can exist. * * *

"Our care should be to bring her (the Republic) back to her old and safe anchorage." * * *

"It is amid these gloomy surroundings and sad forebodings, gentlemen of the Historical Society, that we who have not lost all hope and faith, are met to take counsel together. We may be able, it is true, to save but little from the general wreck, but we can, at least, leave to future generations the true record of our struggle in a righteous cause." * * *

This society proposes to publish regularly and systematically all contributions which elucidate the truth, reflect the glory, and maintain the principles, involved in the late war, and it calls upon all who are not lost to honor, to aid in this laudable undertaking. It wishes to enrol not only every true man, but every true woman in its ranks. * * *

"Maid, mother, wife, gave freely to that country the most cherished objects of their affections. * * * It was wisely done, therefore, to invoke their aid in behalf of our society. * * * It is theirs to teach our children that their fathers were neither traitors nor rebels; that we believed as firmly as in the eternal word of God that we were in the right; and that we have a settled faith which no trials can shake, that, in His own good time, the right will be made manifest."

"These are the lessons our children should learn from their mothers. Nor are these the only ones which should be inculcated, for the pages of history furnish many which should not be overlooked. These teach in the clearest and most emphatic manner, that there is always hope for a people who cherish the spirit of freedom, who will not tamely give up their rights, and who, amid all the changes of time, the trials of adversity, remain steadfast to their convictions that liberty is their birthright. * * * When Napoleon in that wonderful campaign of Jena, struck down in a few weeks the whole military strength of Prussia, destroyed that army with which the great Frederic had held at bay the conbined forces of Europe, and crushed out, apparently forever, the liberties, seemingly the very existence of that great State, but one hope of her disenthrallment and regeneration was left her—the unconquered and unconquerable patriotism of her sons. As far as human foresight could penetrate the future this hope appeared but vain and delusive one; yet only a few years passed before her troops turned the scale to victory at Waterloo, and the Treaty of Paris atoned in part for the mortification of that of Tilsit. * * * She educated her children by a system which made them good citizens in peace and formidable soldiers in war; she kindled and kept alive the sacred fire of patriotism; she woke the slumbering spirit of the Fatherland; and what has been the result of this self devotion of a whole people for half a century? Single-handed she has just met her old antagonist; the shame of her defeats of yore has been wiped out by glorious victories; the contributions extorted from her have been more than repaid; her insults have been avenged and her victorious eagles sweeping over the broken lillies of her enemy, waved in triumph from the walls of conquered Paris, while she dictated peace to prostrate and humbled France. Is not the moral to be drawn from this noble dedication of a people, to the interests and honor of their country, worth remembering? * * *

"Hungary in her recent struggle to throw off the yoke of Austria was crushed to the earth, and, yet, to-day the Hungarians, as citizens of Austria, exercise a controlling power in that great empire. * * *

"Mr. President and gentlemen of the Society, the task assigned to me by your partial kindness has been discharged. * * * It seemed to me not inappropriate while explaining the purposes of the Society, to show to you how important are the objects it contemplates, how vital to the future condition of our people, and how vast the influence it may exercise if properly directed. History repeats itself, and history is philosophy, teaching by examples. If the examples presented to you have kindled any zeal in behalf of your suffering country, if they have inspired in your hearts any ray of hope for its redemption, my efforts have not been in vain."

Liberal quotations have been made from the speech of Hampton, because he spoke for the Southern Historical Society. He was chosen by that society to explain its purposes, and the speech was published by the society in its official organ, (the *Southern Magazine*, Baltimore, Md., January, 1874.) It was not made in moments of excitement before an enthusiastic and tumultuous crowd, but it was carefully prepared to present to the Southern people the purposes of the society, and it was delivered before some of the ablest generals of the Confederacy. The language of Hampton is strong and clear, and no one can doubt his meaning, and he was speaking for such men as Jefferson Davis, Early, Beauregard, Semmes, Fitzhugh Lee, Governor Letcher, Hunter, Hood, and other able leaders of the Confederacy. Before the war, he was one of the wealthiest of the slave lords. The language of such a man, at such a time, endorsed by a society composed of such men, should be carefully pondered by the American people.

The sense and force of Hampton's argument is that the North and South constitute two different peoples—"antagonistic sections"—that the South fought for liberty, and was crushed; but her people can regain their liberty, as Prussia did, by war, and to that end her sons should be so educated as to make them "good citizens in peace, and formidable soldiers in war;" or they may control the Republic as the statesmen of Hungary control the Austrian Empire.

DAVIS AND EARLY.

It is evident that Jefferson Davis is in ascord with the members of this society, some of whom were among his ablest lieutenants in the struggle to destroy the nation; and they received him as "the President"—of the Confederacy, of course.

Jubal Early, the president of the society, is one of the most extreme and bitter of the Bourbon leaders.

THE MAJORITY OF THE SOUTHERN PEOPLE NOT THE DISLOYAL.

It is not believed that a majority of the Southern people are disloyal, but it is believed that a large majority of the slave aristocracy entertain the views expressed by Hampton. These slave lords who ruled the South and the Nation before the war, seek to do so again. True they are but a small minority of the Southern people, yet they are by reason of their thorough organization, singleness of purpose, superior education, wealth and desperation, the absolute masters of the Southern Democracy.

THE PEOPLE BEING EDUCATED BY THE SLAVE LORDS.

Since 1873, they have been preparing the minds of the people for the great struggle of of 1876. The speech of Gen. Preston, at the University of Virginia, was one of the steps in the process of educating the people. Similar speeches have been made elsewhere.

THE BOURBON PLAN TO GAIN THE CONTROL.

As far as developed, the plan of the Bourbon leaders appears to be to control the electoral vote of every Southern State, with the hope of receiving enough votes from Northern States to elect a President who will allow them to "retain the old plantation system, or, in lieu of that, establish a baronial one." If they control the 138 electoral votes of the Southern States, and they probably will, 46 votes from the North will give them the President.

There are reasons for believing that many liberal Democrats will refuse to follow the Bourbon leaders, when their purposes are fully understood. It is proper, perhaps, in this connection, to allude to the labors of Bishop Kavanaugh, Dr. Clark, and other pastors of the Southern Methodist Church, in favor of fraternal union with the Northern Methodist Church. It is true that their's is purely a Christian work, but they are followed by many earnest Christians in the South, both pastors and laymen, who are Democrats, but not Bourbons, and it is believed that they will refuse to follow the Bourbon leaders. Many believe that the split in the Methodist Church in 1844, prepared the way for secession in 1861. May not the fraternal union of the great Methodist family lead to the fraternal union of the Northern and Southern people? I shall again allude to this subject.

A Georgia Republican.

CHAPTER IV.

GEORGIA TO LEAD IN THE COMING GREAT STRUGGLE BETWEEN STATE SOVEREIGNTY AND NATIONAL SUPREMACY—THE CONFEDERATE ASSOCIATION OF GEORGIA—TREASONABLE SPEECH OF BEN HILL.

Savannah, Ga., August 27, 1875.

It is believed that Georgia will take the lead in the "coming great struggle" between State sovereignty and national supremacy, as South Carolina did in the former great struggle. But it is not believed that the Georgia leaders will pursue the same policy that the South Carolina leaders did, though the struggle will be a determined and desperate one. As I said in a former letter, it may be bloodless; it may be bloody. The people of the North should not be deceived by the Southern Democratic gushers who go North to mislead them. They should ascertain how the representatives of the men who do the "solid voting" act and talk here. The resolute and unflinching men who lead the Southern Democracy will press their purposes inexorably. They will not hesitate to *crush* their opponents, if they can, and it is policy to do so. It is important therefore to fully understand their purposes.

THE SOUTHERN HISTORICAL SOCIETY ORGANIZED IN GEORGIA.

The Atlanta *Constitution*, of January 16, 1874, published an address of Henry Eubank, "General Agent, Southern Historical Society," to the people of Georgia, in which he said:

"But it is not only for the securing, before it is too late, the materials for a true history of the war that the Southern Historical Society will, in its legitimate operations, become an instrumentality of incalculable benefit to the South. Having enrolled among its members the true exponents of Southern honor and intelligence, it will necessarily possess a vitality, and exert a moral influence through the whole South, which will steadily and irresistibly expand into an antagonism, powerful to repel the insiduous advances of those vicious principles which are now so fearfully undermining the civilization of the North. * * *

"In view of the vital issues involved, and the noble results attainable through the effective operations of this society, I dare not doubt the success of my efforts in Georgia in its behalf."

The plain English of the above is, that the organization of the Southern Historical Society will repel the advance of Republican principles in the South.

On the 18th of February, 1874, a State branch of the Southern Historical Society was organized in Atlanta. General A. H. Colquitt, "Vice President for the State of Georgia for the parent Society," presided. "A number of distinguished ex-Confederate generals were present." Branch societies were then organized in Augusta, and other cities in Georgia. Soon there were reunions of the "men who stood shoulder to shoulder in the days that tried men's souls." First there were reunions of companies, then of regiments and brigades.

THE CONFEDERATE ASSOCIATION ORGANIZED.

In November, 1874, a call was issued, signed by Generals Gordon, Benning, Young, Gartrell, and over two thousand other "soldiers of the late army of the Confederate States," for a convention to meet in Atlanta, on the 20th of January, 1875, to organize an association to be known as "The Survivors' Association of Confederate soldiers of the State of Georgia." They gave the following reasons, among others, for organizing the society:

"We are assured in our minds that much of the evil consequent upon our late unhappy war has arisen from a demoralization of the public sentiment of the intrigues of unscrupulous politicians, and (we are) desirous again to infuse into the public mind and heart such a spirit as will enable the posterity of those who secured American independence and constitutional government in the revolution of 1776, to preserve the same from the spoilation of mere jobbers in politics."

The convention met at the appointed time, and organized an association, as proposed. The following officers were chosen:

President—General Joseph E. Johnston; Senior Vice-President—General A. R. Lawton; Vice-Presidents—Generals Robert Toombs, Lafayette McLaws, J. B. Gordon, A. H. Colquitt, H. L. Benning, C. A. Evans, Philip Cook, H. R. Jackson, P. M. B. Young, L. J. Gartrell, D. M. Dubose, R. H. Anderson.

The objects of the society, as set forth in the preamble to the Constitution, are: "To perpetuate the memories which bound us together in the past; to preserve the record of our actions; to care for the widows and orphans of comrades in arms who have filled patriot graves, *and to guard by all peaceful means those principles for which we fought.*" The italics are mine.

THE TREASONABLE SPEECH OF BEN HILL.

By request of the Convention, Ben Hill delivered an address, which was received "with the wildest applause" by "the men who stood shoulder to shoulder in the days that tried men's souls." The following extracts from his speech will show what he supposed the purposes of the organization to be. He said:

"Secession was a mistake, a terrible mistake: but secession was no crime. (Great applause.) It violated no oaths; it trampled upon no individual rights. * * * It sought to shed no blood! Radicalism is no mistake. It is deliberate, intentional, wicked, ever increasing crime. (Applause.) It has trampled upon ten thousand oaths to support the Constitution. It defied the Union as a fact, that it might destroy the Union as a principle, under the pretence of reconstructing the States. I arraign radicalism to-night before the bar of this outraged country as the only real, intentional rebel in American history. (Applause.) It is a rebel against the Constitution of our fathers. It is a rebel against the sovereignty of States. * * * It is a rebel against every principle of justice, and a rebel against every blessing of liberty. (Tremendous applause.) * * *

"The great and final struggle to settle the question whether Constitutional liberty on this continent shall be continued or not is to be fought in 1876. Can it be successfully fought at the ballot-box? * *

"I want the mind of the American people directed to one inquiry! It is a great inquiry, a glorious inquiry. Oh! I look forward to the discussion with real rapture! Who in American history is a rebel? Is it a man who tramples upon the Constitution, or a man who simply resents such infidelity by seeking to get away from such a party? * * *

"Fellow-citizens: I look to the contest of 1876 not only as the most important that ever occurred in American history, but as the most important in the history of the world. * * * If we fail with the ballot-box in 1876 by reason of force, a startling question will present itself to the American people. I trust we will not fail. * * * The indications are in our favor. * * * The great question, and the only question behind for the thought is the one that must be propounded, and for which there is no escape. The question is, is the Constitution of our fathers worth blood? Will you have war or despotism? Will you have blood or empire? That is the question. * * * I tell you my friends there is no peace for this country until Radicalism is crushed! not only crushed but despised; not only despised but made infamous forever throughout America. (Tremendous applause and cheers.) * * * Let us now everywhere in the South habitually speak of the Constitution and the Union under it, with that old reverence and love that distinguished us in the days that are past and gone. I say to-night, there was not a single hour in American history, when the Southern heart was not true to the Constitution. (Applause.) * * *

"If we must have war—if we cannot preserve this Constitution and Constitutional government by the ballot; * * * if the war must come; * * * if inordinate love of power shall decree that America must save her Constitution by blood, let it come. I am ready. (Enthusiastic applause and cheering.) But let one thing be distinctly understood, that, if another war should come, we of the South will rally under the old flag of our fathers. (Wild applause.) It always was our flag. We were never faithless to it and our enemies were never faithful to it." (Applause.)

THE SIGNIFICANCE OF HILL'S SPEECH.

It was not a wild adventurer who thus addressed the Convention of Confederate soldiers, some of whom were among the foremost generals of the Confederacy; but it was the ablest orator in the South, who has been elected a representative in the Congress of the United States. It will not be denied that he is one of the ablest and most popular Democrats in Georgia.

On the 27th of January, the executive committee of the "Survivors' Association," issued an address "to the surviving soldiers and sailors of the Confederate States army and navy, resident in Georgia," requesting them in each county to call a meeting, and have enrolled all who desire to become members of the association, and forward the rolls to Atlanta, the headquarters of the association, where a consolidated roll is to be made out. These rolls were sent to the Democratic ordinaries, judges of probate; nearly all the ordinaries in Georgia are Democrats who have assisted in the organization of these Confederate associations.

Thus are the people educated for what Stephens calls the "coming great struggle between Constitutionalism and Centralism in the United States," which Ben Hill regards as the most important in the history of the world. It is hoped that the friends of the Union will realize its importance before it is too late. A GEORGIA REPUBLICAN.

The Confederates in the Forty-fourth Congress—Who They Are and What They Did in the Effort to Destroy the Union.

In the following list will be found the names of those who served in the Confederate army. There are a few who from modesty, or perhaps with a dim perception of the fitness of things, do not parade their treason, but the younger men are quite ready to emblazon the act:

Ex-Confederate Officers.

No.	NAMES.	States.	Rank.
	SENATORS.		
1	Goldthwaite. . . .	Ala. . .	Adj't Gen.
2	Jones.	Fla. . .	Brig. Gen.
3	Gordon.	Ga. . . .	Major Gen.
4	Alcorn (Rep). . . .	Miss. . .	Brig. Gen.
5	Cockrell.	Mo. . .	Major Gen.

Ex-Confederate Officers—Continued.

No.	Names.	State.	Rank.
6	Ransom	N. C.	Major Gen.
7	Key	Tenn.	Lieut. Col.
8	Maxey	Texas.	Major Gen.
9	Withers	Va.	Colonel.
	REPRESENTATIVES.		
10	Williams	Ala.	Major
11	Bradford	do.	Colonel.
12	Hays, (Rep)	do.	Brig. Gen.
13	Hewitt	do.	Colonel.
14	Forney	do.	Brig. Gen.
15	Lewis	do.	Colonel.
16	Gause	Ark.	Colonel.
17	Slemons	do.	Brig. Gen.
18	Gunter	do.	Colonel.
19	Smith	Ga.	Captain.
20	Hartridge	do.	Colonel.
21	Cook	do.	Brig. Gen.
22	Blackburn	Ky.	Lieut. Col.
23	Gibson	La.	Brig. Gen.
24	Ellis	do.	Captain.
25	Levy	do.	Colonel.
26	Lamar	Miss.	Colonel.
27	Hooker	do.	Colonel.
28	Franklin	Mo.	Captain.
29	Clark	do.	Brig. Gen.
30	Yeates	N. C.	Major.
31	Waddell	do.	Lieut. Col.
32	Davis	do.	Captain.
33	Scales	do.	Brig. Gen.
34	Robbins	do.	Colonel.
35	Vance	do.	Brig. Gen.
36	Dibrell	Tenn.	Brig. Gen.
37	Whitthorne	do.	Colonel.
38	Atkins	do.	Lieut. Col.
39	Young	do.	Colonel.
40	Culbertson	Texas.	Colonel.
41	Throckmorton	do.	Brig. Gen.
42	Douglas	Va.	Major.
43	Cabell	do.	Colonel.
44	Tucker	do.	Captain.
45	Hunton	do.	Brig. Gen.
46	Ferry	do.	Brig. Gen.
47	Faulkner	W. Va.	Colonel.

The following tables are significant, and should be preserved for future reference:

I. *Ex-Members of the Rebel Government and Congress.*

Present position.	Names.	State.	Position.	Senate.	House.
H. R.	Stephens	Ga.	V. Pres.		
H. R.	Reagan	Texas	P. M. Gen.		1
H. R.	Hill	Ga.		1	
Sen.	Caperton	W. Va.		2	
H. R.	Ashe	N. C.		3	2
H. R.	House	Tenn.			3
H. R.	Goode	Va.			4
H. R.	Smith	Ga.			5
H. R.	Hatcher	Mo.			6
H. R.	Singleton	Miss.			7

II. *Members of Congress before the Rebellion.*

Stephens	Ga.	House.	36th Cong.
Lamar	Miss.	House.	36th Cong.
Singleton	Miss.	House.	36th Cong.
Scales	N. C.	House.	35th Cong.
Atkins	Tenn.	House.	35th Cong.
Reagan	Texas.	House.	36th Cong.
Faulkner	W. Va.	House.	35th Cong.
Harris	Va.	House.	36th Cong.

III. *State and other positions held during the Rebellion.*

Caldwell	Ala.			‡Solicitor
Norwood	Ga.		1†	
Candler	Ga.		2†	
Tucker	Va.			‡At'y Gen
Culberston	Texas.		3†	
Reagan	Texas.	1*		
Stephens	Ga.	2*		
Harris	Ga.	3*	4†	
Candler	Ga.	4*		
Slemons	Ark.	5*		
Gunter	Ark.	6*		
Lamar	Miss.	7*		
Hatcher	Mo.	8*		
Dibrell	Tenn.	9*		
Goode	Va.	10*		
Hunton	Va.	11*		
Harris	Va.	12*		

* Secession Conventions. † State Legislatures. ‡ Legal.

In order that the facts may be fully understood, it is necessary to state that no name is presented in the foregoing tables, other than of those who announce their antecedents in the Congressional Directory, a work compiled by Major Ben. Perley Poore, clerk of printing records, under the direction of the Joint Committee on Printing, or whose records are shown by the Confederate war records now in the archives of the War Department. The authority is quoted in the following extracts from the sources above stated, and from others.

ALABAMA.—*Senator* GEORGE GOLDTHWAITE, of Montgomery; was adjutant general of the State of Alabama during the war.

2d District—Representative JEREMIAH N. WILLIAMS, of Clayton; entered the Confederate army in 1861 as major.

3d District—Rep. PAUL BRADFORD, of Talladega; served in the Confederate army throughout the war.

5th District—Rep. JOHN H. CALDWELL, of Jacksonville; was elected solicitor for the tenth judicial circuit by the legislature, at the session of 1859-'60; re-elected at the session of 1863-'64. This statement shows that he was an officer of the rebel State government, and also of President Johnson's reactionary movement.

6th District—Rep. GOLDSMITH W. HEWITT, of Birmingham; entered the Confederate army in 1861, and served until severely wounded at the battle of Chickamauga in 1863.

At Large—Rep. WILLIAM HENRY FORNEY, of Jacksonville; entered the Confederate army at the commencement of hostilities in 1861, as captain, and was successively promoted major, lieutenant-colonel, colonel and brigadier-general; surrendered at Appomattox C. H.: was a member of the State senate of Alabama 1865-'66, (under the Johnson provisional government.)

At Large—BURWELL BOYKIN LEWIS, of Tuscaloosa; served in the Confederate army as an officer in the Second Alabama cavalry.

ARKANSAS—*1st District—Rep.* LUCIEN C. GAUSE, of Jacksonport; entered the Confederate army in 1861, and served throughout the war, attaining the rank of colonel.

2d District—Rep. WILLIAM F. SLEMONS, of Monticello; was a member of the Arkansas State (secession) convention in 1861; entered the Confederate army in July, 1861, and served through the war. He was a brigade commader under Fagan in the campaign against Steele, in April, 1864, at Poison Springs, near Camden, Ark., when nearly two hundred men belonging to the First Kansas colored (79th U. S. C. T.) regiment were murdered after being wounded or surrendering. He was also in the campaign under Price, in September and October, 1864, by which Western Missouri and Kansas were invaded and partly desolated. The atrocities perpetrated were numerous. An account of them may be found in a rebel book published at Cincinnati, entitled "Shelby and His Men"—the author of which served with Slemons, and in the "Army of the Border," by R. J. Hinton, and "The Annals of Kansas," by D. W. Wilder, State Auditor of Kansas.

4th District—THOMAS MONTICUE GUNTER, of Fayetteville; was a delegate from Washington county in the Arkansas State Convention of May, 1861; served in the Confederate army as colonel Thirteenth Arkansas volunteers. He was also in Fagan's command.

FLORIDA—*Senator* CHARLES W. JONES; was born in Ireland. He was a brigadier-general in the Confederate army, as the Confederate War Department records establish.

GEORGIA—*Senator* THOMAS MANSON NORWOOD, of Savannah; was a member of the Georgia (rebel) legislature in 1861-'62.

Senator JOHN B. GORDON, of Atlanta; at the beginning of the war entered the Confederate army as captain of infantry, and was promoted major, lieutenant-colonel, colonel, brigadier-general, major-general, and to the command of the second army corps; commanded one wing of General Lee's army at Appomattox Court-House; was wounded in battle eight times.

1st District—Rep. JULIAN HARTRIDGE, of Savannah; delegate to the Charleston Democratic Convention in 1860; was in the Confederate army during first year of the war; was a member of the Confederate Congress.

2d District—Rep. WILLIAM E. SMITH, of Albany, entered the Confederate army as a volunteer, in the Fourth Georgia Volunteers, after the State seceded; was elected captain in April, 1862; lost a leg in the defence of Richmond, at King's School House, June 25, 1862; was elected to the Confederate Congress in 1863.

3d District—Rep. PHILIP COOK, of Americus; was elected to the State Senate of Georgia, in 1863 (rebel); was elected a member of the State Convention of 1865, called by President Johnson; entered the Confederate service in 1861, as a private; was commissioned first lieutenant, lieutenant-colonel, colonel, and in August, 1863, brigadier-general.

4th District—Rep. HENRY R. HARRIS, of Greenville; was a member of the Georgia (secession) Convention of 1861.

5th District—Rep. MILTON A. CANDLER, of Atlanta; was a member of the State (rebel) House of Representatives in 1861-'63; of the State Constitutional Convention in 1865—the body called by President Johnson.

8th District—Rep. ALEXANDER HAMILTON STEVENS, of Crawfordsville; was elected to the Secession Convention of Georgia in 1861; opposed and voted against the ordinance of secession in that body, but gave it his support after it had been passed by the convention against his judgment as to its policy; was elected by that convention to the Confederate Congress which met at Montgomery, Alabama, February 4, 1861, and was chosen vice-president under the Provisional government by that Congress; was elected vice-president of the Confederate States for the term of six years under what was termed the permanent government, in November, 1861; visited the State of Virginia on a mission under the Confederate Government in April, 1861, upon the invitation of that State; was one of the commissioners on the part of the Confederate Government at the Hampton Roads' Conference in February, 1865; was elected a Representative to the Twenty-eighth, Twenty-ninth, Thirtieth, Thirty-first, Thirty-second, Thirty-third, Thirty-fourth and Thirty-fifth Congresses, when he declined a re-election; was elected to the Senate of the United States in 1866, by the first legislature convened under the new Constitution (the Johnson provisional movement), but was not allowed to take his seat.

9th District—Rep. BENJAMIN H. HILL, of Atlanta; was a member of the Confederate States Senate, and of the Georgia Secession Convention of 1861.

KENTUCKY—*7th District—Rep.* JOSEPH C. S. BLACKBURN, of Versailles; entered the Confederate army in 1861, and served throughout the war. It is charged that his service was almost wholly that of a guerilla, engaged in hanging the Unionists of Kentucky.

LOUISIANA—*1st District—Rep.* RANDALL LEE GIBSON, of New Orleans; joined the Confederate army as a private soldier, and was promoted to the command of a company, regiment, brigade and division.

2d District—Rep. E. JOHN ELLIS, of New Orleans; graduated in March, 1861; joined the Confederate army five days afterward, and served throughout the war.

4th District—Rep. WILLIAM M. LEVY, of Natchitoches; was a member of the State legislature of Louisiana in 1861; was a Presidential elector on the Breckenridge and Lane ticket in 1860; served in the Confederate army, participating in the engagements on the peninsula in 1861 and 1862, and thereafter, until the close of the war, in the adjutant and inspector general's department on the staff of General Dick Taylor.

MISSISSIPPI—*1st District—Rep.* LUCIUS Q. C. LAMAR, of Oxford; was elected to the Thirty-fifth and Thirty-sixth Congresses of the United States, and resigned in 1860 to take a seat in the Secession Convention of his State; in 1861, entered the Confederate army as lieutenant-colonel of the Nineteenth regiment, and was promoted to the colonelcy; in 1863, was entrusted by President Davis with an important diplomatic mission to Russia.

4th District—Rep. OTHO R. SINGLETON, of Canton; was a representative from Mississippi in the Thirty-third, Thirty-fifth and Thirty-sixth Congresses of the United States, retiring January 12, 1861; was a representative from Mississippi in the Confederate Congress from 1861 until 1865.

MISSOURI — *Senator* F. M. COCKRELL, of Warrensburg; entered the Confederate army as a colonel in the Missouri State Guard, and was promoted to major-general, serving till the rebellion closed.

4th District—Rep. ROBERT A. HATCHER, of New Madrid; was a member of the State (rebel) convention in 1862, and a member of the Confederate Congress in 1864-'65.

8th District—Rep. BENJAMIN J. FRANKLIN, of Kansas City; entered the Confederate army as a private, was promoted captain, and served throughout the war.

11th District—Rep. JOHN B. CLARK, Jr., of Fayette; at the commencement of the late war he entered the Confederate army as a lieutenant, and was promoted successively to be captain, major, colonel and brigadier-general. Clark served in Marmaduke's division, and was a brigade commander in the Price raid of 1864.

NORTH CAROLINA — *Senator* MATT W. RANSOM, of Northampton county (post office Weldon); entered the Confederate army, serving as lieutenant-colonel, colonel, brigadier-general and major-general and surrendered at Appomattox.

Senator AUGUSTUS SUMMERFIELD MERRIMON, of Raleigh; was a member of the legislature of North Carolina in 1860-'61; was solicitor (rebel) of the 8th judicial district of North Carolina from 1861 to 1865.

1st District—Rep. JESSE J. YEATES, of Murfreesboro'; served in the Confederate army, and was major of the 31st regiment North Carolina troops; was solicitor (rebel) of the 1st judicial circuit of North Carolina from 1861 to 1866.

3d District—Rep. ALFRED MOORE WADDELL, of Wilmington; served in the Confederate army as lieutenant-colonel of cavalry.

4th District—Rep. JOSEPH J. DAVIS, of Louisburg; served in the Confederate army as captain.

5th District—Rep. ALFRED MOORE SCALES, of Greensborough; was a member of the Thirty-fifth Congress; volunteered at the beginning of the late civil war as a private in the Confederate army; was afterward promoted and served as captain, colonel and brigadier-general, and for the war.

6th District—Rep. THOMAS SAMUEL ASHE, of Wadesborough; was elected in 1861 to the House of Representatives of the Confederate States, and to the Senate of the Confederate States in 1864.

7th District—Rep. WILLIAM M. ROBBINS, of

Statesville; was an officer in the Confederate army during the whole war.

8th District—Rep. ROBERT BRANK VANCE, of Asheville; was elected a captain of a company in the Confederate service in 1861; was twice elected colonel of the 29th North Carolina regiment, and was appointed brigadier-general in 1863.

TENNESSEE—*Senator* DAVID MCKENDREE KEY, of Chattanooga; entered the Confederate army in 1861, and served through the entire war.

3d District—Rep. GEORGE GIBBS DIBRELL, of Sparta; was elected to the State (rebel) legislature of Tennessee, in August, 1861; entered the Confederate army as a private, was elected lieutenant-colonel, and promoted colonel and brigadier-general of cavalry; was detailed to escort the executive officers and treasurer of the Confederate government after the evacuation of Richmond.

4th District—Rep. HAYWOOD YANCEY RIDDLE, of Lebanon; entered the Confederate army as a private in 1861, and served through the war.

6th District—Rep. JOHN F. HOUSE, of Clarksville; was a member of the Provisional Congress of the Confederate States from Tennessee; at the expiration of his term of service in said body, he entered the Confederate army, and continued therein until the close of the war.

7th District—Rep. WASHINGTON CURRAN WHITTHORNE, of Columbia; was assistant adjutant general in the Provisional army of Tennessee in 1861, and was afterward adjutant general of the State, which position he held under Governor Harris until the close of the civil war.

8th District—Rep. JOHN D. C. ATKINS, of Paris; was lieutenant-colonel of the 5th Tennessee regiment in the Confederate army in 1861; was elected to the Confederate Provisional Congress in August, 1861; was re-elected in November, 1861, and again elected in November, 1863.

10th District—Rep. CASEY YOUNG, of Memphis; entered the Tennessee army as a private; was afterward appointed assistant adjutant general upon the staff of Gen. William H. Carroll, and was subsequently assigned to the command of a regiment of cavalry in General Chalmer's division. He also served under Forrest, at the time of the massacre of Fort Pillow.

TEXAS—*Senator* SAM BELL MAXEY, of Paris; educated at West Point, was elected State Senator, for four years, in 1861, but declined, and raised the 9th Texas infantry for the Confederate States army, of which he was colonel; was promoted to brigadier-general in 1862, and major-general in 1864; commanded the Indian Territory military district 1863-65, and was also superintendent of Indian affairs.

1st District—Rep. JOHN H. REAGAN, of Palestine; was elected in 1857 a representative to the Thirty-fifth Congress from the first district of Texas, and was re-elected in 1859 to the Thirty-sixth Congress; was elected to the secession convention of Texas in 1861, and was elected, with others, by that convention, deputy to the Provisional Congress of the Confederacy; was appointed postmaster-general of the Provisional Government of the Confederacy, March 6, 1861; was re-appointed on the permanent organization of the Confederate government in 1862, and occupied the position until the close of the war; was also appointed acting secretary of the treasury of the Confederate government.

2d District—Rep. DAVID B. CULBERSON, of Jefferson; was a member of the State House of Representatives of Texas (rebel) in 1866, and to the State Senate (Johnson) 1866; entered the Confederate army as a private in 1862, and was promoted until he became adjutant general with the rank of colonel.

3d District—Rep. JAMES W. THROCKMORTON, of McKinney, elected to the State (rebel) Senate in 1863, and served until the surrender of General Lee; was elected a delegate to the State Constitutional Convention under President Johnson's proclamation, and was chosen presiding officer of that body; was elected Governor of Texas in June, 1866, for a term of five years; was inaugurated August 8, 1866, and removed by order of General Sheridan, August 9, 1867.

VIRGINIA—*Senator* ROBERT E. WITHERS, of Wytheville; entered the Confederate army as major of infantry in April, 1861, and during the same year was promoted colonel of the 18th Virginia regiment, which he commanded until retired in consequence of numerous disabling wounds, and appointed to command the post at Danville, Virginia, which position he held until the close of the war.

1st District—Rep. BEVERLY B. DOUGLAS, of Ayletts; entered the Confederate army as first lieutenant in Lee's Rangers, and was successively promoted to the rank of major of the 5th Virginia cavalry.

2d District—Rep. JOHN GOODE, Jr., of Norfolk; was elected in 1860 a member of the State (Secession) Convention of Virginia, which passed the ordinance of secession; was twice elected a member of the Confederate Congress, and served in that capacity from February 22, 1862, until the close of the war; was appointed a member of the National Democratic Executive Committee in 1868, and reappointed in 1872 for four years.

5th District—Rep. GEORGE C. CABELL, of Danville; volunteered as a private soldier in the southern army; in June, 1861, he was commissioned major by Governor Letcher, and assigned to the 18th Virginia infantry, Colonel Withers, Pickett's division, Longstreet's corps; participated in most of the battles fought by that portion of the army of Northern Virginia to which he was attached; was twice wounded, and left the army at the close of the war with the rank of colonel.

6th District—Rep. JOHN RANDOLPH TUCKER, of Lexington; was attorney-general of Virginia from 1857 to 1865. Is also borne as a captain on the Confederate army rolls.

7th District—Rep. JOHN T. HARRIS, of Harrisonburg; was a member of the Thirty-sixth Congress of the United States; was a member of the Confederate Legislature from 1863 to '65.

8th District—Rep. EPPA HUNTON, of Warrenton; was elected to the State Convention of Virginia, which assembled at Richmond in February, 1861; served through its first session, and then entered the Confederate army as colonel of the 8th Virginia infantry; was promoted after the battle of Gettysburg, and served through the residue of the war as brigadier-general.

9th District—Rep. WILLIAM TERRY, of Wytheville; was in the military service of Virgina in the "John Brown raid," in 1859; entered the Confederate army in April, 1861, as lieutenant in the 4th Virginia infantry, "Stonewall Brigade," and served during the war.

WEST VIRGINIA—*Senator* ALLEN TAYLOR CAPERTON of Union; was a member of the State (Secession) Constitutional Convention of Virginia in 1861; was elected by the legislature of Virginia a member of the Confederate States Senate, and served until the close of the war in 1865.

2d District — Rep. CHARLES JAMES FAULKNER, of Martinsburg; was elected to the House of Representatives in the Thirty-second, Thirty-third, Thirty-fourth and Thirty-fifth Congresses, serving from December 1, 1851, until March 3, 1859; was nominated in 1859 by President Buchanan as Minister Plenipotentiary to France, and confirmed by the Senate; returned to the United States in August, 1861, and was held as a prisoner of state upon no charge or imputation against his fidelity as a minister, but from an apprehension that he would unite his fortunes with those of the Southern Confederacy; was exchanged in December, 1861, for Hon. Alfred Ely, member of the United States House of Representatives from New York, then a prisoner in Richmond; entered the Confederate army as a member of General Stonewall Jackson's staff, and served as his chief of staff until the death of that officer, having written all the official reports that bear his signature.

www.ingramcontent.com/pod-product-compliance
Lightning Source LLC
LaVergne TN
LVHW010834120826
845149LV00016B/1374

* 9 7 8 1 4 1 8 1 8 9 5 2 5 *